The *Air* I Breathe

PAT GREENLEAF JAMES

THE AIR I BREATHE

Copyright © 2016

Unless otherwise indicated all scripture references are
from the New King James Version

ISBN: 978-1533678683

Printed in the USA

To my husband, the Reverend Larry D. James;
children - Larry (Jamie) and Leah;
grandchildren – Jayd, Laryn, Landon, Dylen &
Masyn. May you forever be aware that God –
The Air I Breathe, *is with you no matter what!*

I love you deeply!

THE AIR I BREATHE

Table of Contents

Foreword

In my vocation as a pastor and spiritual practitioner, I have found in persons who live by a faith and belief in the spiritual realm of life, there exists an influence that exceeds the natural and embraces the mystical, the supernatural. This presence provides interesting results when it comes to overcoming fears, coping with difficult circumstances, displaying emotional resilience from devastating life events, healing, recovery, and restoration from illnesses and terminal diseases.

How we view the world speaks volumes about how we live our lives, how we make decisions, how we view ourselves in the context of life as we believe it to be. One's "world view", defines how and where one fits in the full scheme of existence among all creation, both earthly and spiritual.

In fact, how we live our earthly lives is quite often, if not always, predicated on and dictated by our spiritual view of existence.

During the past twenty-five years in ordained pastoral ministry, I have visited with and counseled countless numbers of individuals who live their daily lives facing the uncertainties of the future... economic depression, global warming and its potential implications, world violence, broken relationships, abuse, sickness and disease, hopelessness.

Many say if it were not for their spiritual beliefs that inform and supply a declared faith and hope above what the earthly life presents, they would live in constant and certain fear of demise.

Studies show that a change in mindset, such as the way we think or the way we view life, has the power to alter neuro chemistry in the brain, producing positive thoughts and actions in the way we respond to circumstances. Those with a sense of belief and expectation (key elements of **hope**) release natural chemicals in the brain (endorphins).

Endorphins produce significant effects that can mimic the effects of the painkilling drug, morphine; thus, reducing pain in the body. Therefore, one's physical condition can be impacted by a mind to body connection (hope and positive thinking), creating a body to mind connection (healing).

This paradigm brings us face to face in a potential crisis where we discover the depth of our faith, our belief, our hope in something, someone outside ourselves.

Howard Thurman, in "The Inward Journey" says, "We discover a religious-spiritual question of the total meaning of life at its heart. We discover for ourselves the depth of our world view; our reliance on our spiritual view that defines our true relationship to **God**, whose **Presence** makes itself known in our most lucid moments of self-awareness."

It is through this Presence of which Thurman speaks that I connect with the author's shared experience in this memoir, *"The Air I Breathe."* It is this **Presence**, this **Spirit**, this **Breath** that gives meaning to faith, belief, and hope when crisis comes to call.

It is this author's 15 days of life-threatening events that gave life to fear, question to mortality, then ultimately provided a miraculous response of life to both. This author opens the door and allows us to enter in and experience firsthand the fragility of life that finds security in the rescuing arms of faith and hope.

My personal sharing of those 15 days with the author has shed a greater light on this woman of profound faith. She is a forward looker and mover of unbridled hope; an unapologetic believer in the **ONE** who daily breathes into her His **Air... Breath... LIFE.**

Beyond those 15 days of shared experience with this author, she and I share an even deeper and more intimate relationship. I live with and love this author as I have for forty-five years. I have experienced up close and personal, how she practices her faith. Her belief and hope makes possible what seems impossible; makes visible what seems invisible; makes movable what seems unmovable.

She is my wife, the love of my life and the one with whom I share the breath of life.

If you are experiencing a crisis in your life, facing a hardship that appears unbearable, facing days of darkness that appear hopeless, it is my hope that as you read this memoir, you will be inspired to seek and trust the life-giving Breath of God. Keep believing, keep hoping, keep the faith; know that this too shall pass.

Larry D. James, M.Div.

Preface

Ever since I can remember, I was the child always ready to take the world by storm. I was prepared to conquer whatever stood in my way, and I was not afraid to face anything. I believed that one must have this attitude in order to be a successful individual. This mindset has contributed to me becoming the person I am today.

At age seven, it was apparent I was strong-willed and determined to be the best in every endeavor. I was competitive, inquisitive, talkative, highly energetic, and a talented singer. Singing has been a significant part of my life since I was four years old. It is God's gift to me that I use to bless Him as I minister in song to others. It has been a privilege to perform in countless churches, civic events, and theaters. I even performed in Tokyo, Japan and was a guest concert artist in Florence, Italy.

When my gift became threatened by having to be placed on a respirator, I announced with shallow breath, "I am a singer and I expect to still have the ability to sing when the tube is removed!" To be unable to sing would be a devastating blow for me.

Because I have always been strong, independent, and assertive, being vulnerable created tremendous discomfort; it made me feel fragile, which is an unnatural feeling for me. It is difficult for things to be "out of my control," and much of this derives from childhood when I was constantly reminded, *you have to be a big girl, and big girls do not cry. You are the one in charge, and you have to be responsible.*

Additionally, I was the caretaker for my younger siblings and cousins. In my mind, I was a grown-up at eleven years of age. Even when we played games, I was always the adult. If we played "school", I was never the student, but rather the principal. I was never afraid to speak up for myself and frequently was a spokesperson for others who were uncomfortable expressing their feelings.

This character trait became an integral part of my adult life, but unfortunately, being the person everyone depends on – for whatever reason – can eventually take a toll on anyone.

Confessing that being out of control makes me uncomfortable has become cathartic as I share this story. This, along with being extremely vulnerable during my illness, serves as a reminder that I am not invincible nor do

I have to be Superwoman; it's all right to cry, and I am not responsible for everyone. Several years ago, I attended a women's prayer breakfast where the speaker encouraged the participants to "Go to your places of vulnerability. God will meet you there."

What a profound and meaningful statement!

Both my husband Larry and daughter Leah, helped me remember this, and I am thankful because it allowed me to rely on others when I needed to. It feels great knowing it is acceptable to be vulnerable because God always has a plan to comfort us.

Life has a way of coming full circle.

The experiences of my illness challenged me to the highest degree. I eventually regained enough mental capacity to act and speak, after only being able to write in the air with colossal mittens on my hands as if playing charades. It was during this moment when I began to focus on changing my present circumstances through prayer and total dependence on God.

The pages of this book were written to share a personal experience and to remind us that there is hope in every life encounter. Further, this book serves as an inspirational tool for those who may be suffering, who may have lost their way, and for those who feel they have no hope. Having hope provides the ability to embrace life in a positive way, even during our darkest times. Even in my darkest moments, it never occurred to me I would not emerge victorious.

It is my sincere desire this story will inspire and encourage you if you are struggling, or if your purpose is to encourage others.

Acknowledgements

I am infinitely grateful for the encouragement and support received from my husband, The Reverend Larry D. James, M.Div., who kept daily notes of conversations with medical staff for future reference. Your love and wisdom have guided me every step of the way. You were, and have always been my calming assurance in every situation.

I am grateful to my son, Larry (Jamie) James, a man of God who knows the power of prayer; my daughter, Leah James, a kind and compassionate soul who also knows how to pray and provided invaluable input, as well as, my daughter-in-law, Dylesha James, who took time to accompany me during medical procedures during my illness.

I appreciate my lifelong friends, Dawn Payne who is also a medical professional, and my high school friend, Harriette Richard, Ph.D. Their encouragement has propelled me forward in this project.

I thank my grandson Landon for his assistance in ensuring that I worked on this project each day.

I would be remiss should I not acknowledge my siblings, many family members and in-laws, who rallied prayer warriors on my behalf.

I am equally grateful for the doctors and nurses at Carolina Medical Center and Carolyn Bradshaw – a great friend, who tenderly cared for me during my crisis.

To my loving Grier Heights Presbyterian Church family, The Presbytery of Charlotte, NC; friends from Antioch Baptist Church in Charlotte, New Liberation Presbyterian Church of San Francisco, CA, Gaines Street Baptist Church of Little Rock, AR, friends of the Little Rock Community Choir, the Men's Chorus from Ebenezer Baptist Church, Atlanta, GA, Sorors of the Alpha Lambda Omega Chapter of Alpha Kappa Alpha, Inc., neighbors and friends from near and far who prayed for me constantly – THANK YOU!

Last, but certainly not least, I thank three amazing friends for their assistance: Harriette Richard, Kimberly Malone, and Gerry Wallace. Your commitment, insight and support have been phenomenal!

THE AIR I BREATHE

By Pat Greenleaf James

The finger of God touches the air I breathe.
Its gentle breeze envelopes me in peace,
I find rest in the air I breathe.

The air I breathe secures and keeps me safe.
It soothes my doubts and calms my deepest fears,
The air I breathe comforts me.

The air I breathe is healing.
It permeates every fiber of my being,
I am made whole by the air I breathe.

Trust in the LORD with all your heart,
And lean not on your own understanding;
In all your ways acknowledge Him,
And He shall direct your paths.

~Proverbs 3:5-6

Introduction

The Lord has done great things
whereof we are glad.
~Psalm 126:3

I have a condition known as Waldenstrom's Macroglobulin Anemia – a lymphoma uncommon to African Americans. I was diagnosed in 1992, and until recently, I managed it well. In 2004, after 12 years of taking an oral chemotherapy drug and relocating to another state, my new oncologist decided that a new treatment plan was necessary.

The new treatment was administered via a port in my hand and lasted for a period of three months. This seemed to suffice for the moment, though remission was nowhere in sight.

Fortunately, I was able to continue working and doing other things I loved. Having a positive outlook on life was and still is a tremendous driving force.

After the initial scare and uncertainty about Waldenstrom's, I never thought much about it. I trusted God with this problem I was unable to handle. Many people, family included, were unaware anything was wrong; I looked and acted healthy, and thank God – I still do!

During the initial years of living with this disease, God worked through me in enormous ways I would have never imagined. In 1996, we relocated from Atlanta to San Francisco, immersing ourselves in new territory, jobs, friends, etc., learning to bloom where God planted us.

After getting over the shock of moving so far away from the familiar, I became excited about this new adventure. Waldenstrom's was still very active and finding a new physician was a priority.

It did not take long to get back in the swing of my medication regimen; 23 pills taken once per month on Fridays.

Those Friday nights and Saturdays were for nausea and vomiting; Sundays were spent at church directing the choir, as usual. This was the pattern until we moved to Charlotte in 2004, where I began a new treatment plan.

In the eight years we lived in San Francisco, I was able to achieve much success despite Waldenstrom. During this period, I received the Mayor's Excellence in Teaching

Award, organized and led numerous international student tours, and wrote and recorded two songs.

I share this not to boast, but show how amazing God was despite my circumstances. His grace is sufficient to supply all we need when we trust and depend on him.

I was determined to not be defeated by my situation!

The Dreaded Stairs

My help comes from the Lord,
who made heaven and earth.
~Psalm 121:2

As we rode through the neighborhood – after 15 days of hospitalization – every house looked new. Lawns and shrubbery were green and tenderly manicured, and Knockout Roses were in full bloom; returning home never felt more wonderful.

I arrived home to the delight of beautiful flowers that friends had planted for me. With the beauty and glamour that greeted me upon entering the neighborhood, I could never have imagined the terror waiting inside my house; the dreaded stairs... all 15 of them!

The first day home was calming, finally getting a break from the frequency of medical staff coming in to perform the required regimen of vitals and medications.

As night approached, I was terrified of climbing the stairs to our bedroom. My grandson, Landon, eagerly jumped up to assist me.

He was on my left side and my loyal husband, Larry, was on the right, guiding me through this exhausting pilgrimage of the dreaded stairs.

After what seemed like an eternity, we finally reached the top. I was so dizzy; I had to lie on the floor to regain enough strength to continue my journey to the bed.

This process and agony of walking one step at a time persisted for two weeks. On several occasions, Larry literally lifted me to carry me up the stairs. After two weeks of torture, I was finally able to negotiate the stairs alone – a simple act often taken for granted.

Thank God for the blessings of the simple things in life.

Rewind

I shall not die, but live,
and declare the works of the Lord.
~Psalm 118:17

In March 2013, I received a call from the oncologist's office insisting that I have an immediate blood infusion – a six-hour procedure – so I went in the next day. Two weeks later, I had to have a second infusion and became very concerned.

The necessity of these procedures explained why I was tired more than usual for a Type A individual such as myself.

After the second infusion, I began a new form of chemotherapy that lasted five months. I continued working every day and did my chemotherapy in the late afternoons twice per week. This new drug worked extremely well during the initial treatments, but it had a short-lived effect.

In September, I received news that a more aggressive form of chemotherapy was necessary, and that I wouldn't be able to continue working. This was devastating news because work meant everything to me! I was a committed and dedicated professional, and I believed in the service I provided each day to students and other colleagues. I was good at what I did, and the word retirement had never been in my thoughts or vocabulary.

April 29, 2014 was an ordinary day. The sun illuminated the sky as I made my way to a much-needed dental appointment to have three infected teeth extracted. After many months of chemotherapy, my immune system had become severely compromised, which caused the delay of necessary dental work.

I waited one year for this appointment simply because my white and red blood cell count was too low to have done it sooner. This experience became the precursor to a 15-day hospital stay partially spent in ICU on a respirator. My immune system was vulnerable, creating an "open season" for alien invaders on my body.

Three days after having the infected teeth removed, I noticed several lesions disseminated in my face and several other locations on my body. I returned to the dental surgeon's office thinking it may be related to the surgery; it was not. While I was there, they noticed my blood pressure was at an extremely dangerous level, and my chest felt as though an anvil was sitting on it.

The dentist instructed me to return to my oncologist's office for further evaluation. From there, I was sent to the emergency room and subsequently admitted to the hospital where numerous medical procedures were performed.

Two nodules were detected on one of my lungs, but they could not determine why. After three days, I was sent home. By the end of the week, I was crawling in the floor and my chest was still hurting. I returned to the hospital for re-admission and several specialists were summoned for further consultation.

What initially were two nodules had now multiplied and infiltrated both my lungs. The doctors were baffled and requested yet another specialist.

It was shingles... in my lungs! To add to the severity of this very rare case of shingles, pneumonia was diagnosed, necessitating admission to the Intensive Care Unit (ICU). I was placed on a respirator and feeding tube shortly after.

This was a harrowing experience; I felt like I was in the Twilight Zone!

▢

Places Unfamiliar

Yea, though I walk through the valley of the shadow of
death, I will fear no evil; For You are with me;
Your rod and Your staff, they comfort me.
~Psalm 23:4

Being in the hospital was a unique experience with far reaching impact. I have always felt in control of every situation in my personal life, but this experience proved I was not and became the challenge of a lifetime. I chose to remain prayerful, faithful, and positive while assessing this new state of being. I did not know how or when, but I chose to believe I would overcome this place of unfamiliarity.

I love earrings! I wear them sun up to sun down, daily; and I was wearing earrings when admitted to the hospital.

After being admitted so spontaneously, things seemed to spin out of control, which provided little time to think before I was intubated. Hours later when I woke up, I recognized I was not wearing my earrings and signaled for a writing instrument and paper.

When they were provided to me, I wrote, "Where are my earrings? Please put them back on." The medical staff looked puzzled, but laughed about it and honored my request.

My thoughts were just because I was ill, I did not have to appear that way, and I was fighting hard to avoid feeling so. It is my belief that my recovery began at that point.

Several nights while in ICU, I dreamed, or hallucinated, of people passing through my room, which was indeed strange. Each of them was decoratively dressed in antique gold clothing; their eyes were filled with sadness, and they did not speak. I was frightened because I did not understand why they were passing through my room, or who they were.

Were they dead? Was I dead, or dying? Where were they going?

I wanted to ask them, but chose not to as I began to realize it *had* to be a figment of my imagination induced by medication, and I did not have to be afraid.

God was there with me in this unfamiliar place, every step of the way during my journey.

☐

It Ain't Over

I would have lost heart, unless I had believed that I would see the goodness of the LORD in the land of the living.
~Psalm 27:13

After settling into my healing regimen, new obstacles introduced themselves accompanied with the worst pain I had ever experienced. This assailant attacked the left side of my face with a sharp pain that lasted 45-60 seconds. The attacks occurred five to six times daily with a pain so intense that I would just scream in agony with no idea what was happening, or why.

I immediately returned to my primary care physician who, with quick assessment, identified the culprit as trigeminal neuralgia – a chronic pain condition that affects the trigeminal or 5th cranial nerve (as defined by the National Institute of Neurological Disorders and Stroke).

With the prescription of yet another medication, added to the existing regimen, I was able to manage this new menace and begin my healing journey.

Illness can bring great uncertainty of life, particularly when it seems you will never get well or feel normal again. It is during times like this our reliance on God deepens and our prayers must become more fervent. Prayer gives us strength for the journey, and is the focus of my favorite passage of scripture that comes from Psalm 121:

I will lift up my eyes to the hills—
From whence comes my help?
My help comes from the LORD,
Who made heaven and earth.
He will not allow your foot to be moved;
He who keeps you will not slumber.
Behold, He who keeps Israel
Shall neither slumber nor sleep.
The LORD is your keeper;
The LORD is your shade at your right hand.
The sun shall not strike you by day,
Nor the moon by night.
The LORD shall preserve you from all evil;
He shall preserve your soul.
The LORD shall preserve your going out and your
coming in
From this time forth, and even forevermore.

This passage has been a pacifying source of comfort for me throughout the years and provided further assurance that I was not alone; God was with me through every stormy trial and situation.

Face Time

Breath is Spirit. The act of breathing is Living.
~Author Unknown

Recently I learned how to FaceTime in order to communicate with my four grandchildren who live out-of-state.

I was extremely excited and so were my grandchildren.

Our youngest, two-year-old grandchild prefers FaceTime versus talking on the phone, because he is still learning to talk and likes to see who he is "talking" to.

While reading my daily devotion one morning, the writer referred to the fact that we must have "FaceTime with God" to receive instructions for daily living. At that moment, it became abundantly clear that God was moving in me through His Holy Spirit. It further reminded me that I must have FaceTime with God, not only every day, but throughout the day as well.

As Christians, we often become swallowed-up in our daily routines and become slack in our FaceTime with God.

FaceTime with God provides us with daily instruction and brings peace in the midst of our storms.

We must be intentional in our thoughts about God; who He is and what He promises us, His children. We must remember His grace is sufficient for all we need when we trust Him completely. God is able to navigate the circumstances of our lives.

Living with a chronic illness requires that I remain prayerfully positive, and time alone with God is essential to the healing process. I have learned to deeply appreciate getting up early mornings and having that alone FaceTime with God. Because I had such difficulty breathing on my own while hospitalized, my daily mantra has become, "God, thank you for the air I breathe." I have realized I cannot take a single breath for granted. My personal FaceTime begins at this moment, and I know God looks forward to this precious time.

Breathe on me breath of God,
Fill me with life anew.
That I may love what Thou dost love,
And do what Thou wouldst do.
>   -Hymn by Robert Jackson, 1860-1914☐

Faultless Faith

Faith is permitting ourselves to be seized
by the things we do not see.
~Martin Luther

I have always felt I could face any obstacle; bad news, disappointment, illness, etc. Even in the midst of dealing with a chronic disease such as Waldenstrom's, I often locked it in the back of my mind as if to say, *No big deal.* Once I got over the initial shock, my faith kicked in to high gear.

I recall the early days of diagnosis during the second bone marrow procedure – the first did not yield the required results. While sitting in Outpatient Surgery waiting to be checked in, I was thinking and mentally saying, "Lord, I am walking through the valley of the shadow of death, and I am afraid, yet I know you are with me and I trust you completely."

That was 24 years ago.

Faultless faith is faith that experiences, endures, and overcomes the many obstacles we face in life. It moves us to a place of total dependence on God – a place of no return because there is no place else to go.

While doctors searched for a diagnosis, I experienced a promenade of specialists in the quest to determine what was going on in my body. The specialists were as follows: Endocrinologist, Rheumatologist, Neurologist, Hematologist, and finally, Oncologist.

Yes, my symptoms were in alignment in each of these categories. The diagnostic process took one and one half years before a final determination was established.

Somebody gave Superwoman kryptonite!

Fueled by faith, I continued working every day, served as music director at the church my husband pastored, and engaged in many other activities – even when in pain.

The actual diagnosis was so uncommon for African Americans at the time that it was impossible to explain, so I did not try, not even to my family. Only my spouse and a very loyal, lifelong friend who was in the medical profession knew about my condition.

My oncologist had only three other patients diagnosed with Waldenstrom's Macroglobulin Anemia, and they were older Caucasian adults living in rural areas.

As if he had not noticed, I advised him I was, "None of the above" – we both found the humor in this statement. At that moment, my faith spiraled into an even higher realm I refer to as faultless faith.

Faultless faith provides the will to keep going even when it seems like tomorrow will be our last day – and it may. Nevertheless, greater still, God has given us a faith that can move mountains, and I prefer this brand of faultless faith.

"Joy" Girl

*We are shaped by our thoughts; we become
what we think. When the mind is pure, joy follows like a
shadow that never leaves.*
~Buddha

Psalm 30:5 states, *Weeping may endure for a night, but joy comes in the morning.* Several years ago while I was in my late twenties, an elderly woman asked, "Do you ever have any problems? You are always smiling and so friendly."

This was such a strange question for me to be asked.

Even at that tender age, I realized life was not a ray of sunshine every day, but I made the choice to treat my life as though it was. From the time I was diagnosed to my current state of affairs, I have many friends and associates who do not have the slightest notion I have a life-threatening illness, and that I almost died in May 2014.

Once I felt comfortable enough to share my health issues, I was careful with whom I would share it. I did not want pity or sympathy, but prayer and joining of faith, hope, and love. Due to my sometimes over-exuberant personality, I had difficulty accepting my illness – especially the severity of it.

My character reflects that of a funny, witty, and highly energetic Type A individual. I consider myself the "joy" girl; it feels better and certainly produces healthier living. Being joyful takes a conscious effort, and it's important to avoid the joy robbers of life – whether they are people or circumstances. Even while imprisoned by a myriad of health professionals, tubes, respirators, and medicine, and experiencing the lack of vocal ability and other mobilizing restraints, I still had the joy of knowing that God was with me every step of the way.

One morning, I awoke from a dream in which I was directing the choir. My hands were in mid-air as I approached each vocal section. The song was Richard Smallwood's, "Jesus, the Center of my Joy".

What a wonderful way to wake up! As I reflected on this dream, it reminded me that joy comes from deep within. There have been many days I had to reach deep into my soul to find and retain the joy God gave me.

Thank God, I found JOY!

Chemo: Friend or Foe?

"I am determined to be cheerful and happy in whatever situation I may find myself. For I have learned that the greater part of our misery or unhappiness is determined not by our circumstance but by our disposition."
~Martha Washington

The human body is a wonderful but complex phenomenon, and though we – for the most part – are born with similar anatomies, our bodies are not identical. Patients have different tolerance levels when undergoing chemotherapy.

A few of the most prominent side effects from the chemotherapy I experienced included numerous cysts on both eyes (requiring surgery), a 30 pound weight loss, balance issues, an extremely compromised immune system, headaches, mood swings, insomnia, neuropathy, and anxiety.

While conversing with a patient during treatment, she mentioned the term "chemo-brain" and we both laughed.

Little did I know that I would soon share a similar story of having chemo-brain, a condition that occurs after one has been on chemotherapy for an extended period of time. New developments seemed to appear on a weekly basis, but these treatments were vital to my continued well-being. Thankfully, the side effects eventually subside when properly managed.

During the course of my illness, I endured five uniquely different chemotherapy drugs: Leukeran, Fludarabine, Velcade, Bendamustine, and Rituximab. These invaders, as I called them, each had their own debilitating affect in terms of how my body reacted to them – some worse than others.

On at least three occasions, I suffered severe reaction to two of these invaders, which hindered my schedule of treatment. At other times, my white blood cell count was too low to receive treatment. This was always devastating news to me as I was desperately seeking healing.

It has been two years since my last chemotherapy treatment, and I am grateful for the courage God gave me to endure.

While I did not look forward to subsequent treatment, I always managed them with a smile. I called these times my crazy-sock days.

Each treatment day, I wore different color mix-matched socks; ranging from bright orange stripes to raspberry and lime green patterns. Not only did the crazy socks make me feel better, but the other patients and medical staff enjoyed them as well.

These crazy socks helped me think of so many reasons to be happy, even in a time of crisis. God always provides a way of escape from the complexities of life – even chemotherapy.

Never Alone

And the LORD, He is the One who goes before you. He will be with you; He will not leave you nor forsake you; do not fear nor be dismayed.

~Deuteronomy 31:8

During my hospital stay, I initially thought I would be there for a few days and then would be able to go home. I understood something was significantly wrong, but I did not realize how serious it really was until specialists kept coming into my room. Before I knew it, I was admitted to ICU and in isolation, thereby resulting in all who entered my room to wear masks and gowns for protection.

Being unable to have visitors created a loneliness I had not experienced before. I believe it was then that I began to painstakingly understand the severity of my condition.

I found myself separated from people I loved most, except for Larry, my husband.

I was all alone, except for the recurring hallucinations of people passing through my room each night.

I felt as though I was in a nightmare!

One day as I reflected on what was happening, God reminded me that I was not alone and that He had been, and would continue to be, with me throughout this season of anguish.

Even those of us with the strongest faith can begin to doubt and feel abandoned when in a situation we cannot control or understand. What an assurance to know that God will never leave nor forsake us!

I love the lyrics of Rogers and Hammerstein's popular song, "You'll Never Walk Alone." This song has tremendous similarity to Psalm 23, offering a declaration of hope and assurance that we indeed never walk alone. I have found this to be true on many occasions during my lifetime.

Actually, this belief drives my faith because God has promised he will not leave us and He has kept His promise throughout time.

When you walk through a storm
Hold your head up high
And don't be afraid of the dark
At the end of the storm
There's a golden sky
And the sweet silver song of a lark
Walk on through the wind
Walk on through the rain
Though your dreams be tossed and blown
Walk on walk on with hope in your heart
And you'll never walk alone
You'll never walk alone.

"You'll Never Walk Alone"
from the 1945 musical *Carousel*
~Rogers and Hammerstein

There is Hope

Hope is faith holding out its hand in the dark.
~George Iles

Family and friends have always thought I could do anything, probably because I told them I could – and I can be pretty convincing. I was that persistent child who never took no for an answer unless forced to do so.

That child blossomed into a full-fledged adult who operated under the same principles. During the early days of diagnosis, I recall literally putting my hands over my ears, because the doctor who was treating me at that time sounded like the voice of doom, and I was not having it.

Though I believe he meant well and was doing the best he could with the information he had, I was neither prepared, nor willing, to accept his doomsday message. On more than one occasion, though I do not recommend this to others, I skipped my appointments.

It was extremely important for me to remain as positive and hopeful as I could, especially after being told there was no cure for my disease. I needed to breathe as I wrapped my head around these new circumstances that threatened my very existence. It would be years before I would be able to accept the fact that I had a chronic illness.

Right now, I am in what the medical professionals refer to as "watchful waiting" mode, and am still being closely monitored.

I call it HOPE!

Recently, my oncologist informed me that the Food & Drug Administration finally approved the drug, Ibrutinib, which was developed to treat patients with Waldenstrom.

Prior to this time, various chemotherapy medications used for a myriad of other cancers and lymphomas had been prescribed.

There is always HOPE!

"You Still Have Hope"

~Author Unknown

If, when faced with the bad, when told everything is futile,
you can still look up and end the conversation with the
phrase... "Yeah... BUT," then you still have hope.
Hope is such a marvelous thing.
It bends, it twists, it sometimes hides, but rarely does it
break.
It sustains us when nothing else can.
It gives us reason to continue and courage to move ahead,
when we tell ourselves we would rather give in.
Hope puts a smile on our face when the heart cannot
manage.
Hope puts our feet on the path when our eyes cannot see
it.
Hope moves us to act when our souls are confused of the
direction.
Hope is a wonderful thing; something to be cherished and
nurtured,
and something that will refresh us in return.
And it can be found in each of us, and it can bring light
into the darkest of places.
Never lose HOPE!

A Work in Progress

Being confident of this very thing, that He who has begun
a good work in you will complete it
until the day of Jesus Christ.
~Philippians 1:6

Retirement had never entered my mind.

I always imagined being the individual they would have to chase from the building. I have held several prestigious and successful positions during my career, but once I became an educator, I believed I had found my niche. However, God was moving me, with little notice, from something I loved – work.

Recently, I ran into one of my former students whom I had not seen for several years. When she learned I had been ill and consequently retired, she was shocked and commented, "Mrs. James, I can't believe it. You have always been that 'jazzy' person with lots of energy, and you don't look as if you've ever been ill!"

It eventually became clear that God was ready for me to move on to something new as He continued to fulfill His divine purpose in me.

I continue to pray for guidance to accept His will – whatever it may be. I have always believed that we move through life on a contingency basis, and this is how we progress. As we grow, we learn new skills, develop new interests, and meet new people. In order to fully mature in Christ, we must learn to bloom where God plants us.

When God chooses to move us from point A to point B, this is when we learn to truly put our trust in Him, as we continue the work He has begun. Though we are not always able to see the end in view, trust the fact that God does.

Two years have transpired since my hospital experience and retirement. As I embrace each new day of life, I continually seek God for my new purpose in life.

I firmly believe each of us has a specific purpose, and it is our responsibility and privilege to look to God in order to discover the reason. There are so many lives to be touched and stories to share with others.

Presently, God is leading me to work with young women who need spiritual mentors. This has been a passion of mine for several years, and I am happy to begin a new ministry titled, "Women in Touch Today," that will launch in the near future.

I continue to receive speaking and singing engagements from various church and civic organizations. In order to assist my healing process, I joined a restorative yoga class at the YMCA, and I feel very refreshed when sessions are completed. I am also an active member of Alpha Kappa Alpha Sorority, Inc.

To God be the glory for the marvelous things He has done!

Our lives do not end with each new setback; these setbacks provide opportunities to begin the next chapter.

I encourage you to begin your next chapter with faith and courage. Each of us has the capacity to make a difference in the lives of others. Trust the fact that God will provide the tools needed for the journey, as we become ambassadors for the cause of Christ.

Today, I stand as a living testimony that through faith and the prayers of the righteous, we *will* reap a great harvest!

Survival Skills...

- *Read daily – this massages the mind*
- *Meditate – this feeds the mind*
- *Pray – eases the mind*
- *Exercise – stimulates the body and mind*
- *Stay positive – increases longevity*
- *Travel the world – adds culture to your life*
- *Learn an instrument – challenges us*
- *Learn a new language – connects us with others*
- *Become a mentor –someone needs you*
- *Volunteer – a good way to meet new friends*
- *Breathe! – it produces LIFE*

Encouragement...

"That if you confess with your mouth the Lord Jesus and believe in your heart that God has raised Him from the dead, you will be saved".

~Romans 10:9

God has a purpose and plan for each of our lives and He loves us so much that He sacrificed His only son, Jesus. Because of this sacrifice, salvation is available to each of us.

Have you accepted His offer?

Sources

Elshof, Phyllis Ten. What Cancer Cannot Do. Stories of Hope and Encouragement. Grand Rapids, MI.

Zondervan. 2006

http://www.ninds.nih.gov/disorders/trigeminal_neuralgia /detail_trigeminal_neuralgia.htm

http://www.brainyquote.com

http://www.artofliving.org

Hammerstein, Oscar and Rogers, Richard. You'll Never Walk Alone. (Original version 1945).

https://tomkinstimes.com/2012/08/youll-never-walk-alone

DHBonner Virtual Solutions LLC
Editing | Cover Design | Interior Layout
www.dhbonner.net

Michael Maxwell Photography
Author Photograph
www.michaelmaxwellphotography.com

CPSIA information can be obtained
at www.ICGtesting.com
Printed in the USA
LVOW10s0504251116

514299LV00007B/69/P